THE WEDDING OF

_____

AND

_____

DATE

_____

Other gift books by Exley:

Wedding Guest Book   Marriage a Keepsake
Our Love Story   Happy Anniversary
A Bouquet of Wedding Jokes The Crazy World of Marriage

BORDER ILLUSTRATIONS BY JUDITH O'DWYER.

Published simultaneously in 1995
by Exley Publications Ltd. in Great Britain,
and Exley Giftbooks in the USA.

12 11 10 9 8 7 6 5 4

Edited by Elizabeth Cotton.
Series Editor Helen Exley.

Copyright © Helen Exley 1995.

ISBN 1-85015-515-1

Designed by Pinpoint Design.
Typeset by Delta, Watford.
Pictures chosen by Helen Exley.
Picture research by P. A. Goldberg and J. M. Clift/Image Select.

Printed in Dubai.

Exley Publications Ltd, 16 Chalk Hill, Watford,
Herts WD1 4BN, United Kingdom.
Exley Giftbooks, 232 Madison Avenue, Suite 1206, New York,
NY 10016, USA.

IMPORTANT NOTE:
For best results we recommend that you
use a fountain pen, a marker or a felt tip
to fill in this book. The pressure of a ball
point pen will show through and spoil
the following pages.

MY WEDDING PLANNER
A Record Book

EDITED BY
HELEN EXLEY

EXLEY
NEW YORK • WATFORD, UK

INTRODUCTION

Your wedding day should be one of the most exciting and enjoyable days of your life, a day that you and your partner will want to share with family and friends, and will remember with pleasure for the rest of your lives!

Planning a wedding, however, can be a daunting prospect – there are endless details to be remembered, lists to be compiled and schedules to be prepared. *My Wedding Planner* is designed to help you keep all the essential details of your wedding plans in one organized place. There is plenty of room for all the lists you will need to make and for recording important telephone numbers, seating plans and other arrangements. At the end of the planner there is a four-month countdown to the big day – so you can make *absolutely* sure that everything runs smoothly right down to the last minute!

The design of this planner is deliberately unstructured, so you can use it to suit whatever style of wedding you have in mind – whether it be simple or elaborate, formal or relaxed. The important thing is that you have the wedding that *you* want.

Filling in this planner will take much of the stress out of the run-up to your big day. Perhaps you'll even find that planning your wedding is as much fun as the day itself! Either way, *"My Wedding Planner"* is not only an invaluable organizer, it is also a beautiful souvenir of your special day.

IMPORTANT NOTE:
For best results we recommend that you use a fountain pen, a marker or a felt tip to fill in this book. The pressure of a ball point pen will show through and spoil the following pages.

Contents

IMPORTANT TELEPHONE NUMBERS

USE THESE PAGES FOR THE TELEPHONE NUMBERS OF ALL
THOSE INVOLVED WITH THE ORGANIZATION OF YOUR
WEDDING, e.g. DRESSMAKER, FLORIST, CATERER, CHAUFFEUR.

NAME:

TEL:

NAME:

TEL:

NAME:

TEL:

NAME:

TEL:

NAME:

TEL:

NAME:

TEL:

NAME:

TEL:

NAME:

TEL:

NAME:

TEL:

NAME:

TEL:

IMPORTANT TELEPHONE NUMBERS

NAME:

TEL:

NAME:

TEL:

NAME:

TEL:

NAME:

TEL:

NAME:

TEL:

NAME:

TEL:

NAME:

TEL:

NAME:

TEL:

NAME:

TEL:

NAME:

TEL:

NAME

TEL:

NAME:

TEL:

NAME:

TEL:

NAME:

TEL:

NAME:

TEL:

NAME:

TEL:

NAME:

TEL:

NAME:

TEL:

NAME:

TEL:

NAME:

TEL:

GUEST LIST

NAME: _____ TEL: _____

ADDRESS: _____

☐ No. ATTENDING CEREMONY

☐ No. ATTENDING RECEPTION

☐ ACCOMMODATION REQUIRED?

GIFT RECEIVED: _____

☐ THANK-YOU SENT

NAME: _____ TEL: _____

ADDRESS: _____

☐ No. ATTENDING CEREMONY

☐ No. ATTENDING RECEPTION

☐ ACCOMMODATION REQUIRED?

GIFT RECEIVED: _____

☐ THANK-YOU SENT

NAME: _____ TEL: _____

ADDRESS: _____

☐ No. ATTENDING CEREMONY

☐ No. ATTENDING RECEPTION

☐ ACCOMMODATION REQUIRED?

GIFT RECEIVED: _____

☐ THANK-YOU SENT

NAME: _____ TEL: _____

ADDRESS: _____

☐ No. ATTENDING CEREMONY

☐ No. ATTENDING RECEPTION

☐ ACCOMMODATION REQUIRED?

GIFT RECEIVED: _____

☐ THANK-YOU SENT

NAME: _____ TEL: _____

ADDRESS: _____

☐ No. ATTENDING CEREMONY

☐ No. ATTENDING RECEPTION

☐ ACCOMMODATION REQUIRED?

GIFT RECEIVED: _____

☐ THANK-YOU SENT

NAME: _____ TEL: _____

ADDRESS: _____

☐ No. ATTENDING CEREMONY

☐ No. ATTENDING RECEPTION

☐ ACCOMMODATION REQUIRED?

GIFT RECEIVED: _____

☐ THANK-YOU SENT

GUEST LIST

NAME:		TEL:
ADDRESS:	☐	No. ATTENDING CEREMONY
	☐	No. ATTENDING RECEPTION
	☐	ACCOMMODATION REQUIRED?
GIFT RECEIVED:	☐	THANK-YOU SENT

NAME:		TEL:
ADDRESS:	☐	No. ATTENDING CEREMONY
	☐	No. ATTENDING RECEPTION
	☐	ACCOMMODATION REQUIRED?
GIFT RECEIVED:	☐	THANK-YOU SENT

NAME:		TEL:
ADDRESS:	☐	No. ATTENDING CEREMONY
	☐	No. ATTENDING RECEPTION
	☐	ACCOMMODATION REQUIRED?
GIFT RECEIVED:	☐	THANK-YOU SENT

NAME:		TEL:
ADDRESS:	☐	No. ATTENDING CEREMONY
	☐	No. ATTENDING RECEPTION
	☐	ACCOMMODATION REQUIRED?
GIFT RECEIVED:	☐	THANK-YOU SENT

NAME:		TEL:
ADDRESS:	☐	No. ATTENDING CEREMONY
	☐	No. ATTENDING RECEPTION
	☐	ACCOMMODATION REQUIRED?
GIFT RECEIVED:	☐	THANK-YOU SENT

NAME:		TEL:
ADDRESS:	☐	No. ATTENDING CEREMONY
	☐	No. ATTENDING RECEPTION
	☐	ACCOMMODATION REQUIRED?
GIFT RECEIVED:	☐	THANK-YOU SENT

NAME: TEL:

ADDRESS:

☐ No. ATTENDING CEREMONY

☐ No. ATTENDING RECEPTION

☐ ACCOMMODATION REQUIRED?

GIFT RECEIVED:

☐ THANK-YOU SENT

NAME: TEL:

ADDRESS:

☐ No. ATTENDING CEREMONY

☐ No. ATTENDING RECEPTION

☐ ACCOMMODATION REQUIRED?

GIFT RECEIVED:

☐ THANK-YOU SENT

NAME: TEL:

ADDRESS:

☐ No. ATTENDING CEREMONY

☐ No. ATTENDING RECEPTION

☐ ACCOMMODATION REQUIRED?

GIFT RECEIVED:

☐ THANK-YOU SENT

NAME: TEL:

ADDRESS:

☐ No. ATTENDING CEREMONY

☐ No. ATTENDING RECEPTION

☐ ACCOMMODATION REQUIRED?

GIFT RECEIVED:

☐ THANK-YOU SENT

NAME: TEL:

ADDRESS:

☐ No. ATTENDING CEREMONY

☐ No. ATTENDING RECEPTION

☐ ACCOMMODATION REQUIRED?

GIFT RECEIVED:

☐ THANK-YOU SENT

NAME: TEL:

ADDRESS:

☐ No. ATTENDING CEREMONY

☐ No. ATTENDING RECEPTION

☐ ACCOMMODATION REQUIRED?

GIFT RECEIVED:

☐ THANK-YOU SENT

GUEST LIST

NAME: TEL:

ADDRESS:

☐ No. ATTENDING CEREMONY

☐ No. ATTENDING RECEPTION

☐ ACCOMMODATION REQUIRED?

GIFT RECEIVED: ☐ THANK-YOU SENT

NAME: TEL:

ADDRESS:

☐ No. ATTENDING CEREMONY

☐ No. ATTENDING RECEPTION

☐ ACCOMMODATION REQUIRED?

GIFT RECEIVED: ☐ THANK-YOU SENT

NAME: TEL:

ADDRESS:

☐ No. ATTENDING CEREMONY

☐ No. ATTENDING RECEPTION

☐ ACCOMMODATION REQUIRED?

GIFT RECEIVED: ☐ THANK-YOU SENT

NAME: TEL:

ADDRESS:

☐ No. ATTENDING CEREMONY

☐ No. ATTENDING RECEPTION

☐ ACCOMMODATION REQUIRED?

GIFT RECEIVED: ☐ THANK-YOU SENT

NAME: TEL:

ADDRESS:

☐ No. ATTENDING CEREMONY

☐ No. ATTENDING RECEPTION

☐ ACCOMMODATION REQUIRED?

GIFT RECEIVED: ☐ THANK-YOU SENT

NAME: TEL:

ADDRESS:

☐ No. ATTENDING CEREMONY

☐ No. ATTENDING RECEPTION

☐ ACCOMMODATION REQUIRED?

GIFT RECEIVED: ☐ THANK-YOU SENT

GUEST LIST

NAME: TEL:

ADDRESS:

☐ No. ATTENDING CEREMONY

☐ No. ATTENDING RECEPTION

☐ ACCOMMODATION REQUIRED?

GIFT RECEIVED: ☐ THANK-YOU SENT

NAME: TEL:

ADDRESS:

☐ No. ATTENDING CEREMONY

☐ No. ATTENDING RECEPTION

☐ ACCOMMODATION REQUIRED?

GIFT RECEIVED: ☐ THANK-YOU SENT

NAME: TEL:

ADDRESS:

☐ No. ATTENDING CEREMONY

☐ No. ATTENDING RECEPTION

☐ ACCOMMODATION REQUIRED?

GIFT RECEIVED: ☐ THANK-YOU SENT

NAME: TEL:

ADDRESS:

☐ No. ATTENDING CEREMONY

☐ No. ATTENDING RECEPTION

☐ ACCOMMODATION REQUIRED?

GIFT RECEIVED: ☐ THANK-YOU SENT

NAME: TEL:

ADDRESS:

☐ No. ATTENDING CEREMONY

☐ No. ATTENDING RECEPTION

☐ ACCOMMODATION REQUIRED?

GIFT RECEIVED: ☐ THANK-YOU SENT

NAME: TEL:

ADDRESS:

☐ No. ATTENDING CEREMONY

☐ No. ATTENDING RECEPTION

☐ ACCOMMODATION REQUIRED?

GIFT RECEIVED: ☐ THANK-YOU SENT

NAME:	TEL:

ADDRESS:		No. ATTENDING CEREMONY
		No. ATTENDING RECEPTION
		ACCOMMODATION REQUIRED?
GIFT RECEIVED:		THANK-YOU SENT

NAME:	TEL:

ADDRESS:		No. ATTENDING CEREMONY
		No. ATTENDING RECEPTION
		ACCOMMODATION REQUIRED?
GIFT RECEIVED:		THANK-YOU SENT

NAME:	TEL:

ADDRESS:		No. ATTENDING CEREMONY
		No. ATTENDING RECEPTION
		ACCOMMODATION REQUIRED?
GIFT RECEIVED:		THANK-YOU SENT

NAME:	TEL:

ADDRESS:		No. ATTENDING CEREMONY
		No. ATTENDING RECEPTION
		ACCOMMODATION REQUIRED?
GIFT RECEIVED:		THANK-YOU SENT

NAME:	TEL:

ADDRESS:		No. ATTENDING CEREMONY
		No. ATTENDING RECEPTION
		ACCOMMODATION REQUIRED?
GIFT RECEIVED:		THANK-YOU SENT

NAME:	TEL:

ADDRESS:		No. ATTENDING CEREMONY
		No. ATTENDING RECEPTION
		ACCOMMODATION REQUIRED?
GIFT RECEIVED:		THANK-YOU SENT

GUEST LIST

NAME:		TEL:
ADDRESS:	☐	No. ATTENDING CEREMONY
	☐	No. ATTENDING RECEPTION
	☐	ACCOMMODATION REQUIRED?
GIFT RECEIVED:	☐	THANK-YOU SENT

NAME:		TEL:
ADDRESS:	☐	No. ATTENDING CEREMONY
	☐	No. ATTENDING RECEPTION
	☐	ACCOMMODATION REQUIRED?
GIFT RECEIVED:	☐	THANK-YOU SENT

NAME:		TEL:
ADDRESS:	☐	No. ATTENDING CEREMONY
	☐	No. ATTENDING RECEPTION
	☐	ACCOMMODATION REQUIRED?
GIFT RECEIVED:	☐	THANK-YOU SENT

NAME:		TEL:
ADDRESS:	☐	No. ATTENDING CEREMONY
	☐	No. ATTENDING RECEPTION
	☐	ACCOMMODATION REQUIRED?
GIFT RECEIVED:	☐	THANK-YOU SENT

NAME:		TEL:
ADDRESS:	☐	No. ATTENDING CEREMONY
	☐	No. ATTENDING RECEPTION
	☐	ACCOMMODATION REQUIRED?
GIFT RECEIVED:	☐	THANK-YOU SENT

NAME:		TEL:
ADDRESS:	☐	No. ATTENDING CEREMONY
	☐	No. ATTENDING RECEPTION
	☐	ACCOMMODATION REQUIRED?
GIFT RECEIVED:	☐	THANK-YOU SENT

PAGE 21

NAME: TEL:

ADDRESS: ☐ No. ATTENDING CEREMONY

                                         ☐ No. ATTENDING RECEPTION

                                         ☐ ACCOMMODATION REQUIRED?

GIFT RECEIVED: ☐ THANK-YOU SENT

NAME: TEL:

ADDRESS: ☐ No. ATTENDING CEREMONY

                                         ☐ No. ATTENDING RECEPTION

                                         ☐ ACCOMMODATION REQUIRED?

GIFT RECEIVED: ☐ THANK-YOU SENT

NAME: TEL:

ADDRESS: ☐ No. ATTENDING CEREMONY

                                         ☐ No. ATTENDING RECEPTION

                                         ☐ ACCOMMODATION REQUIRED?

GIFT RECEIVED: ☐ THANK-YOU SENT

NAME: TEL:

ADDRESS: ☐ No. ATTENDING CEREMONY

                                         ☐ No. ATTENDING RECEPTION

                                         ☐ ACCOMMODATION REQUIRED?

GIFT RECEIVED: ☐ THANK-YOU SENT

NAME: TEL:

ADDRESS: ☐ No. ATTENDING CEREMONY

                                         ☐ No. ATTENDING RECEPTION

                                         ☐ ACCOMMODATION REQUIRED?

GIFT RECEIVED: ☐ THANK-YOU SENT

NAME: TEL:

ADDRESS: ☐ No. ATTENDING CEREMONY

                                         ☐ No. ATTENDING RECEPTION

                                         ☐ ACCOMMODATION REQUIRED?

GIFT RECEIVED: ☐ THANK-YOU SENT

GUEST LIST

NAME: _____ TEL: _____

ADDRESS: _____

□ No. ATTENDING CEREMONY

□ No. ATTENDING RECEPTION

□ ACCOMMODATION REQUIRED?

GIFT RECEIVED: _____

□ THANK-YOU SENT

NAME: _____ TEL: _____

ADDRESS: _____

□ No. ATTENDING CEREMONY

□ No. ATTENDING RECEPTION

□ ACCOMMODATION REQUIRED?

GIFT RECEIVED: _____

□ THANK-YOU SENT

NAME: _____ TEL: _____

ADDRESS: _____

□ No. ATTENDING CEREMONY

□ No. ATTENDING RECEPTION

□ ACCOMMODATION REQUIRED?

GIFT RECEIVED: _____

□ THANK-YOU SENT

NAME: _____ TEL: _____

ADDRESS: _____

□ No. ATTENDING CEREMONY

□ No. ATTENDING RECEPTION

□ ACCOMMODATION REQUIRED?

GIFT RECEIVED: _____

□ THANK-YOU SENT

NAME: _____ TEL: _____

ADDRESS: _____

□ No. ATTENDING CEREMONY

□ No. ATTENDING RECEPTION

□ ACCOMMODATION REQUIRED?

GIFT RECEIVED: _____

□ THANK-YOU SENT

NAME: _____ TEL: _____

ADDRESS: _____

□ No. ATTENDING CEREMONY

□ No. ATTENDING RECEPTION

□ ACCOMMODATION REQUIRED?

GIFT RECEIVED: _____

□ THANK-YOU SENT

GUEST LIST

NAME:	TEL:
ADDRESS:	No. ATTENDING CEREMONY
	No. ATTENDING RECEPTION
	ACCOMMODATION REQUIRED?
GIFT RECEIVED:	THANK-YOU SENT

NAME:	TEL:
ADDRESS:	No. ATTENDING CEREMONY
	No. ATTENDING RECEPTION
	ACCOMMODATION REQUIRED?
GIFT RECEIVED:	THANK-YOU SENT

NAME:	TEL:
ADDRESS:	No. ATTENDING CEREMONY
	No. ATTENDING RECEPTION
	ACCOMMODATION REQUIRED?
GIFT RECEIVED:	THANK-YOU SENT

NAME:	TEL:
ADDRESS:	No. ATTENDING CEREMONY
	No. ATTENDING RECEPTION
	ACCOMMODATION REQUIRED?
GIFT RECEIVED:	THANK-YOU SENT

NAME:	TEL:
ADDRESS:	No. ATTENDING CEREMONY
	No. ATTENDING RECEPTION
	ACCOMMODATION REQUIRED?
GIFT RECEIVED:	THANK-YOU SENT

NAME:	TEL:
ADDRESS:	No. ATTENDING CEREMONY
	No. ATTENDING RECEPTION
	ACCOMMODATION REQUIRED?
GIFT RECEIVED:	THANK-YOU SENT

NAME: TEL:

ADDRESS:

No. ATTENDING CEREMONY

No. ATTENDING RECEPTION

ACCOMMODATION REQUIRED?

GIFT RECEIVED:

THANK-YOU SENT

NAME: TEL:

ADDRESS:

No. ATTENDING CEREMONY

No. ATTENDING RECEPTION

ACCOMMODATION REQUIRED?

GIFT RECEIVED:

THANK-YOU SENT

NAME: TEL:

ADDRESS:

No. ATTENDING CEREMONY

No. ATTENDING RECEPTION

ACCOMMODATION REQUIRED?

GIFT RECEIVED:

THANK-YOU SENT

NAME: TEL:

ADDRESS:

No. ATTENDING CEREMONY

No. ATTENDING RECEPTION

ACCOMMODATION REQUIRED?

GIFT RECEIVED:

THANK-YOU SENT

NAME: TEL:

ADDRESS:

No. ATTENDING CEREMONY

No. ATTENDING RECEPTION

ACCOMMODATION REQUIRED?

GIFT RECEIVED:

THANK-YOU SENT

NAME: TEL:

ADDRESS:

No. ATTENDING CEREMONY

No. ATTENDING RECEPTION

ACCOMMODATION REQUIRED?

GIFT RECEIVED:

THANK-YOU SENT

GUEST LIST

NAME: _____ TEL: _____

ADDRESS: _____

☐ No. ATTENDING CEREMONY

☐ No. ATTENDING RECEPTION

☐ ACCOMMODATION REQUIRED?

GIFT RECEIVED: _____

☐ THANK-YOU SENT

NAME: _____ TEL: _____

ADDRESS: _____

☐ No. ATTENDING CEREMONY

☐ No. ATTENDING RECEPTION

☐ ACCOMMODATION REQUIRED?

GIFT RECEIVED: _____

☐ THANK-YOU SENT

NAME: _____ TEL: _____

ADDRESS: _____

☐ No. ATTENDING CEREMONY

☐ No. ATTENDING RECEPTION

☐ ACCOMMODATION REQUIRED?

GIFT RECEIVED: _____

☐ THANK-YOU SENT

NAME: _____ TEL: _____

ADDRESS: _____

☐ No. ATTENDING CEREMONY

☐ No. ATTENDING RECEPTION

☐ ACCOMMODATION REQUIRED?

GIFT RECEIVED: _____

☐ THANK-YOU SENT

NAME: _____ TEL: _____

ADDRESS: _____

☐ No. ATTENDING CEREMONY

☐ No. ATTENDING RECEPTION

☐ ACCOMMODATION REQUIRED?

GIFT RECEIVED: _____

☐ THANK-YOU SENT

NAME: _____ TEL: _____

ADDRESS: _____

☐ No. ATTENDING CEREMONY

☐ No. ATTENDING RECEPTION

☐ ACCOMMODATION REQUIRED?

GIFT RECEIVED: _____

☐ THANK-YOU SENT

NAME:	TEL:

ADDRESS:

No. ATTENDING CEREMONY

No. ATTENDING RECEPTION

ACCOMMODATION REQUIRED?

GIFT RECEIVED:

THANK-YOU SENT

NAME:	TEL:

ADDRESS:

No. ATTENDING CEREMONY

No. ATTENDING RECEPTION

ACCOMMODATION REQUIRED?

GIFT RECEIVED:

THANK-YOU SENT

NAME:	TEL:

ADDRESS:

No. ATTENDING CEREMONY

No. ATTENDING RECEPTION

ACCOMMODATION REQUIRED?

GIFT RECEIVED:

THANK-YOU SENT

NAME:	TEL:

ADDRESS:

No. ATTENDING CEREMONY

No. ATTENDING RECEPTION

ACCOMMODATION REQUIRED?

GIFT RECEIVED:

THANK-YOU SENT

NAME:	TEL:

ADDRESS:

No. ATTENDING CEREMONY

No. ATTENDING RECEPTION

ACCOMMODATION REQUIRED?

GIFT RECEIVED:

THANK-YOU SENT

NAME:	TEL:

ADDRESS:

No. ATTENDING CEREMONY

No. ATTENDING RECEPTION

ACCOMMODATION REQUIRED?

GIFT RECEIVED:

THANK-YOU SENT

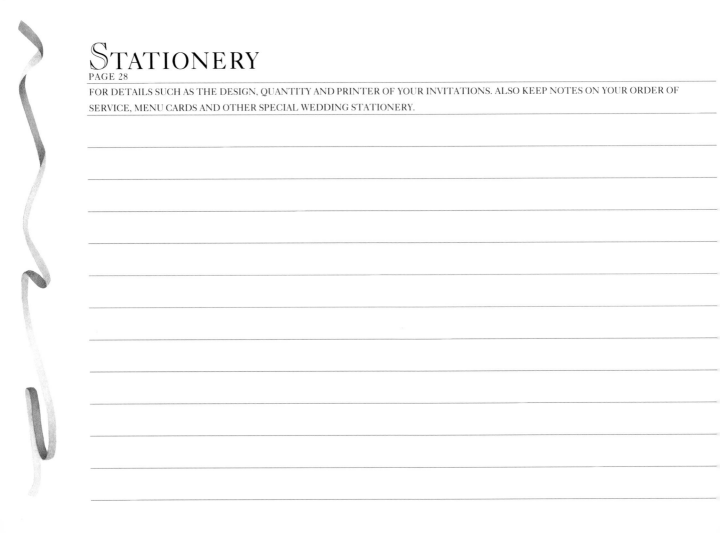

STATIONERY

FOR DETAILS SUCH AS THE DESIGN, QUANTITY AND PRINTER OF YOUR INVITATIONS. ALSO KEEP NOTES ON YOUR ORDER OF SERVICE, MENU CARDS AND OTHER SPECIAL WEDDING STATIONERY.

GIFT LIST

STOCKISTS, SIZES, PRICES AND DETAILS OF THE GIFTS YOU'D MOST LIKE TO RECEIVE.

GIFT LIST

PAGE 32

THE BRIDE'S OUTFIT

PAGE 35

DETAILS OF YOUR DRESS, FITTINGS, DRESSMAKER, VEIL, SHOES, AND DELIVERY DATES. YOU MAY ALSO WANT TO RECORD DETAILS OF YOUR GOING AWAY OUTFIT. DON'T FORGET "SOMETHING OLD, SOMETHING NEW, SOMETHING BORROWED, SOMETHING BLUE"!

THE BRIDE'S OUTFIT

PAGE 36

HAIR AND BEAUTY APPOINTMENTS

THE BRIDESMAIDS' OUTFITS

USE THESE PAGES TO NOTE DETAILS OF YOUR BRIDESMAIDS' SIZES - PLUS DETAILS OF STYLES, FITTINGS AND DELIVERY DATES.

THE GROOM'S OUTFIT

PAGE 40

DETAILS OF SIZES, FITTINGS, TAILOR AND HIRE SHOP.

Best man's and ushers' outfits

DETAILS OF SIZES, FITTINGS, TAILOR OR HIRE SHOP.

OUTFITS FOR OTHER MEMBERS OF THE PARTY

DETAILS OF SIZES, FITTINGS, TAILOR/DRESSMAKER AND HIRE SHOP.

FLOWERS FOR THE BRIDE AND BRIDESMAIDS

USE THIS PAGE TO RECORD DETAILS OF YOUR BOUQUET, YOUR BRIDESMAIDS' FLOWERS AND ANY HAIR ORNAMENTS.

FLOWERS FOR THE WEDDING PARTY

BUTTONHOLE FLOWERS FOR GROOM, BEST MAN AND USHERS, ALSO FLOWERS FOR MOTHERS OF THE BRIDE AND GROOM.

FLOWERS FOR THE CEREMONY/RECEPTION

THE RINGS

PAGE 49

SIZES AND STYLES OF RINGS AND COLLECTION DATES.

THE PHOTOGRAPHS

PAGE 50

LIST THE PHOTOGRAPHS THAT *YOU* WANT TAKEN, ALSO NOTE DOWN GROUPINGS, LOCATIONS AND SCHEDULE.

THE VIDEO

NOTE DOWN THE SCHEDULE AND LIST OF SCENES *YOU* WANT RECORDED.

PRE-WEDDING PARTIES

GUEST LISTS, DATES AND TIMES OF SHOWERS/BRIDESMAIDS' PARTIES, REHEARSAL DINNER, HEN AND STAG PARTIES...

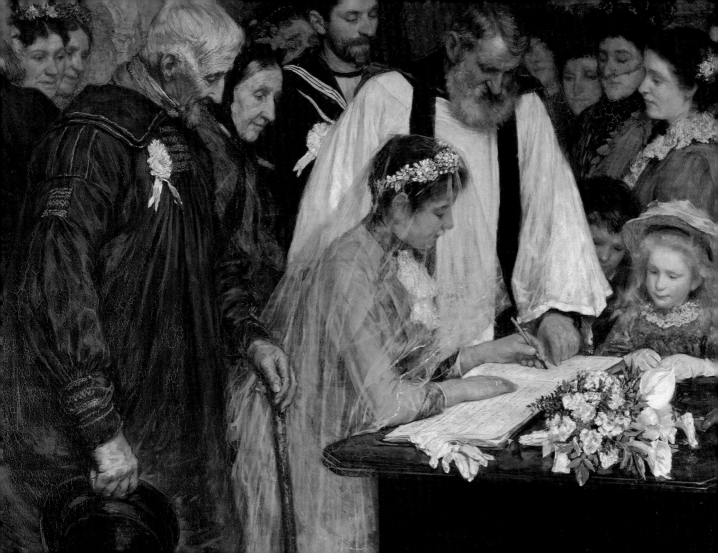

PLANNING THE CEREMONY

RECORD DETAILS OF LOCATION, MUSIC, ANY SPECIAL READINGS THAT HAVE BEEN CHOSEN, DECORATIONS ETC.

THE CEREMONY
PAGE 56

MAKE A BRIEF SCHEDULE, NOTING THE TIMES THAT VARIOUS MEMBERS OF THE WEDDING PARTY AND GUESTS ARE TO ARRIVE.

TRANSPORT
PAGE 58

DETAILS OF TRAVEL ARRANGEMENTS FOR THE MEMBERS OF THE WEDDING PARTY TO THE CEREMONY AND TO THE RECEPTION. ALSO PARKING ARRANGEMENTS FOR GUESTS AT THE CEREMONY AND RECEPTION.

TRANSPORT

TRANSPORT PLANS FOR ANY GUESTS WITHOUT THEIR OWN TRANSPORT.

THE RECEPTION

MAKE A BRIEF SCHEDULE OF EVENTS, INCLUDING WHAT TIME THE WEDDING PARTY IS DUE, ORDER OF RECEPTION LINE, TIME THE MEAL STARTS, TIME OF THE SPEECHES.

SEATING PLAN

YOU CAN USE THESE PAGES EITHER TO LIST NAMES OF GUESTS AT EACH TABLE, OR TO DRAW TABLE PLANS.

TABLE ......   TABLE ......

Seating plan

TABLE ......

TABLE ......

SEATING PLAN
PAGE 64

TABLE ......

TABLE ......

Seating plan

TABLE ......

TABLE ......

Place settings

PAGE 66

FOR NOTES ON ANY SPECIAL TABLE DECORATIONS, CUTLERY, CROCKERY AND TABLE LINEN WHICH ARE REQUIRED.

Menu

THE CHOICE OF DISHES AND NOTES ON VEGETARIAN AND SPECIAL DIETS TO BE CATERED FOR.

DRINKS

QUANTITY AND TYPE OF WINE/CHAMPAGNE AND NON-ALCOHOLIC DRINK REQUIRED FOR RECEPTION.

THE SPEECHES

DETAILS OF THE TIME AND ORDER OF THE SPEECHES AND WHO IS TO GIVE THEM.

THE CAKE
PAGE 72

STYLE, SIZE, WHEN TO BE COLLECTED, CAKE BOXES NEEDED FOR GUESTS UNABLE TO ATTEND.

MUSIC FOR THE RECEPTION

DETAILS OF MUSIC ARRANGED, SCHEDULE AND ANY SPECIAL REQUESTS FOR THE DANCE MUSIC - TELL YOUR DJ OR BAND!.

The honeymoon

ACCOMMODATION FOR WEDDING NIGHT AND HONEYMOON. TRAVEL AGENT'S DETAILS,
DEPARTURE TIMES AND COLLECTION DATES FOR TICKETS.

COUNTDOWN: MONTH 4

THE FOURTH MONTH BEFORE THE WEDDING, DATE ......

1	12	23
2	13	24
3	14	25
4	15	26
5	16	27
6	17	28
7	18	29
8	19	30
9	20	31
10	21	
11	22	

THE THIRD MONTH BEFORE THE WEDDING, DATE ......

12

13

14

15

16

17

18

19

20

0

1

23

24

25

26

27

28

29

30

31

21

22

THE SECOND MONTH BEFORE THE WEDDING, DATE ......

	12	23
	13	24
	14	25
	15	26
	16	27
	17	28
	18	29
	19	30
	20	31
	21	
	22	

THE 4thWEEK BEFORE THE WEDDING

MONDAY

FRIDAY

TUESDAY

SATURDAY

WEDNESDAY

SUNDAY

THURSDAY

NOTES

THE 3rd WEEK BEFORE THE WEDDING

MONDAY

FRIDAY

TUESDAY

SATURDAY

WEDNESDAY

SUNDAY

THURSDAY

NOTES

THE 2nd WEEK BEFORE THE WEDDING

MONDAY

FRIDAY

TUESDAY

SATURDAY

WEDNESDAY

SUNDAY

THURSDAY

NOTES

THE WEEK OF THE WEDDING

MONDAY

FRIDAY

TUESDAY

SATURDAY

WEDNESDAY

SUNDAY

THURSDAY

NOTES

THE DAY BEFORE THE WEDDING

7:00A.M.

1:00P.M.

7:00P.M.

8:00A.M.

2:00P.M.

8:00P.M.

9:00A.M.

3:00P.M.

9:00P.M.

10:00A.M.

4:00P.M.

10:00P.M.

11:00A.M.

5:00P.M.

11:00P.M.

12:00NOON

6:00P.M.

12:00MIDNIGHT

THE WEDDING DAY

7:00A.M.	1:00P.M.	7:00P.M.
8:00A.M.	2:00P.M.	8:00P.M.
9:00A.M.	3:00P.M.	9:00P.M.
10:00A.M.	4:00P.M.	10:00P.M.
11:00A.M.	5:00P.M.	11:00P.M.
12:00NOON	6:00P.M.	12:00MIDNIGHT

NOTES

Acknowledgements

Exley Publications is very grateful to the following individuals and organizations for permission to reproduce their pictures. Whilst all reasonable efforts have been made to clear copyright and acknowledge sources and artists, Exley Publications would be happy to hear from any copyright holder who may have been omitted.

COVER: *The Wedding Morning,* Bacon, Lady Lever Art Gallery/Board of Trustees of the National Museums and Galleries on Merseyside.

OPPOSITE PAGE 1: *Garden in May,* Maria Oakey Dewing (1845-1927), National Museum of American Art, Smithsonian, The Bridgeman Art Library.

PAGE 5: *Attending to the Bride,* Joseph Caraud (1821-1905), Waterhouse and Dodd, London, The Bridgeman Art Library.

PAGE 8: *Woman in an Interior,* Albert Breaute b.1853, Gavin Graham Gallery, London, The Bridgeman Art Library.

PAGE 13: *Domino!,* Frank Bramley (1857-1915), Cork Public Museum, Ireland, The Bridgeman Art Library.

PAGE 17: *Vor Dem Spiegel,* Georg Friedrich Kersting (1785-1847), Archiv Fur Kunst.

PAGE 23: *Woman Ironing,* Edgar Degas (1834-1917), Mr and Mrs Paul Mellon Collection, National Gallery of Art, Washington, Archiv Fur Kunst.

PAGE 30: *Silver,* (detail) 1938, Sir William Nicholson (1872-1949), © 1995 Elizabeth Banks, Tate Gallery, London/Art Resource, N.Y.

PAGE 34: *The Seamstress,* Charles Baugniet (1814-1886), Victoria & Albert Museum, London, The Bridgeman Art Library.

PAGE 38: *Cutting the Cake,* John Strickland Goodall b.1908, Christopher Wood Gallery, London, The Bridgeman Art Library.

PAGE 44: *Spring,* Sir John Lavery (1856-1941), Musee d'Orsay, Paris, Giraudon/The Bridgeman Art Library.

PAGE 48: *Her Wedding Day,* Anton Weiss (1801-1851), Christie's, London, The Bridgeman Art Library.

PAGE 54: *Signing the Marriage Register,* James Charles (1851-1906), Bradford Art Galleries and Museums, The Bridgeman Art Library.

PAGE 60: *The Wedding Meal,* Albert-Auguste Fourie b.1854, Musee des Beaux-Arts, Rouen, The Bridgeman Art Library.

PAGE 67: *Roses and Lilies,* Mary Elizabeth Duffield (1819-1914), by Courtesy of the Board of Trustees of the V&A, The Bridgeman Art Library.

PAGE 70: *Hip Hip Hurrah!* Artists' Party, Skagen, Peter Severin Kroyer (1851-1909), Gotesborg Konstmuseum, Sweden, The Bridgeman Art Library.

PAGE 75: *The Village Wedding,* Sir Luke Fildes (1844-1927), Private Collection, The Bridgeman Art Library.

PAGE 78: *A Floral Composition,* Hubert Bellis (1831-1902), by courtesy of Galerie Berko, Fine Art Photographic Library, Ltd.

PAGE 85: *Woman in her Bath Washing her Leg with Sponge,* Edgar Degas (1834-1917), Musee d'Orsay, Paris, The Bridgeman Art Library.

PAGE 89: *The Bride,* Anders Zorn (1860-1920), Statens Konstmuseer, Stockholm.